This book belongs to:

_____

_____

MW01504221

by:
MoTo Mo

INTRODUCTION

Welcome to the exciting world of motocross! Get ready for a thrilling journey filled with mazes, dot-to-dot challenges, coloring pages, matching games, and complete-the-drawing activities. This Motocross Activity Book is designed especially for young motocross enthusiasts to have fun while learning and improving their cognitive skills.

TABLE OF CONTENTS

1. **Maze Mania:** Help the motocross rider navigate through a tricky maze to reach the finish line. Make sure to avoid obstacles along the way!

2. **Connect the Dots:** Connect the numbered dots to reveal a fantastic motocross scene. The more dots you connect, the clearer the picture becomes!

3. **Coloring Pages:** Use your imagination to color motocross bikes, riders, and thrilling race tracks. Let your creativity run wild with vibrant colors!

4. **Find the Match:** Engage in a fun matching game where you'll pair up exciting motocross-themed images. Can you match them all and become a matching master?

5. **Complete the Drawing:** Start with a half-finished motocross picture and complete it with your own unique design. You're the artist here!

TIPS FOR PARENTS AND CAREGIVERS:

✓ **Supervision:** While this activity book is designed to be fun and educational, adult supervision is recommended, especially for younger children.

✓ **Safety First:** Emphasize the importance of safety when discussing motocross with your child. Highlight the use of helmets, pads, and safe riding practices.

✓ **Encourage Creativity:** Encourage your child to be creative with their coloring and drawing. There are no right or wrong colors in the motocross world!

✓ **Learning Opportunity:** Use this activity book as an opportunity to teach your child about balance, coordination, and problem-solving skills through motocross-themed activities.

✓ **Celebrate Achievements:** Praise your child for their efforts and accomplishments in completing the activities. Motivate them to finish the book and share their creations with family and friends.

CONCLUSION

This Motocross Activity Book offers an engaging and educational way for children to explore the thrilling world of motocross. As they tackle mazes, connect the dots, add color to their favorite riders, match items, and complete drawings, they'll not only have fun but also enhance their cognitive and motor skills. So, grab your markers, pencils, and get ready to embark on a motocross adventure!

MAZE MANIA

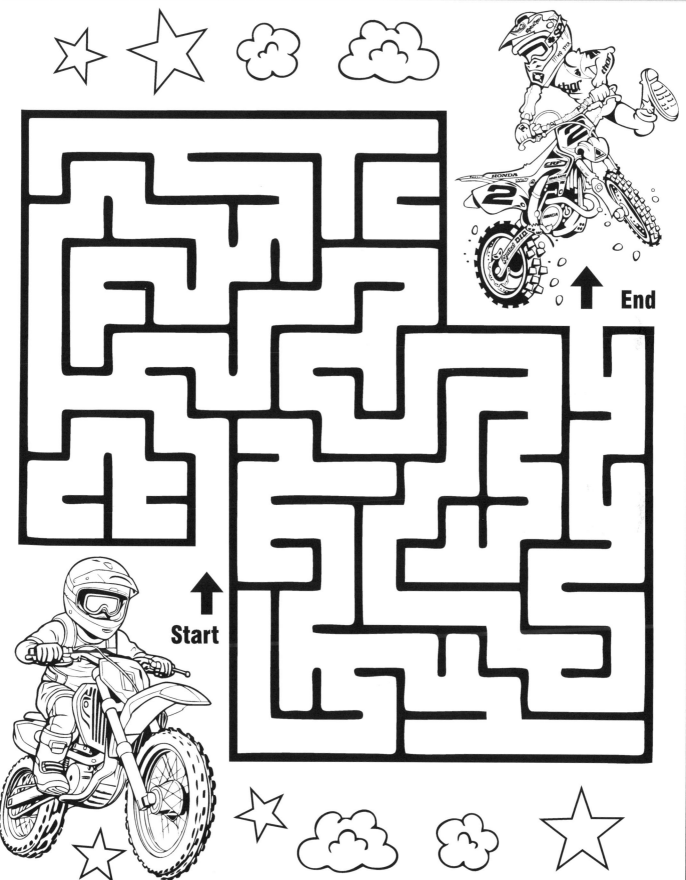

End

Start

CONNECT THE DOTS

FIND THE MATCH

COMPLETE THE DRAWING

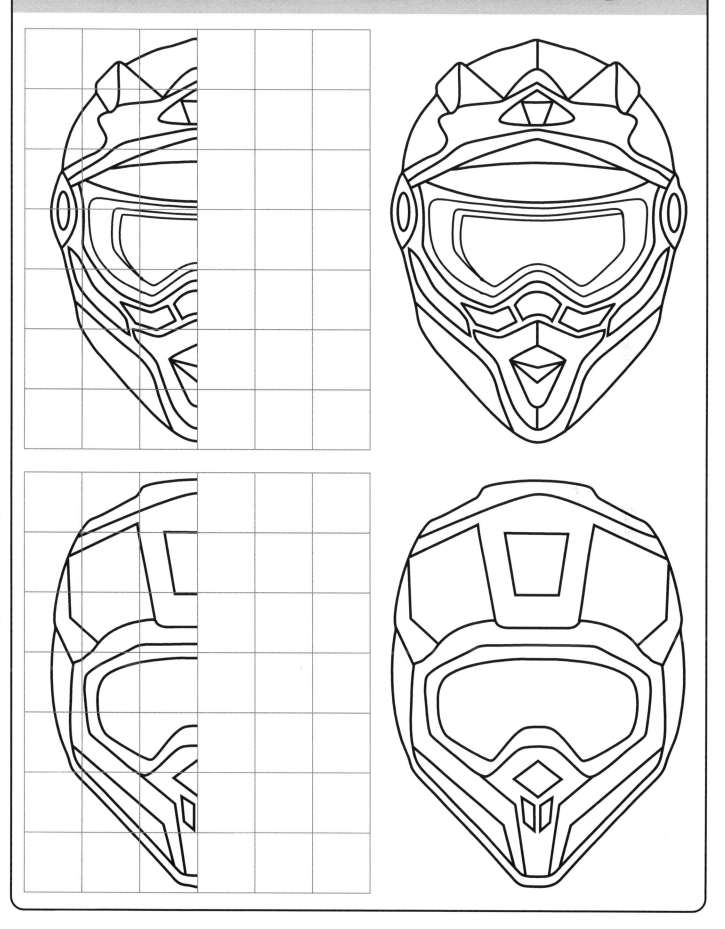

MAZE MANIA

End

Start

58

CONNECT THE DOTS

FIND THE MATCH

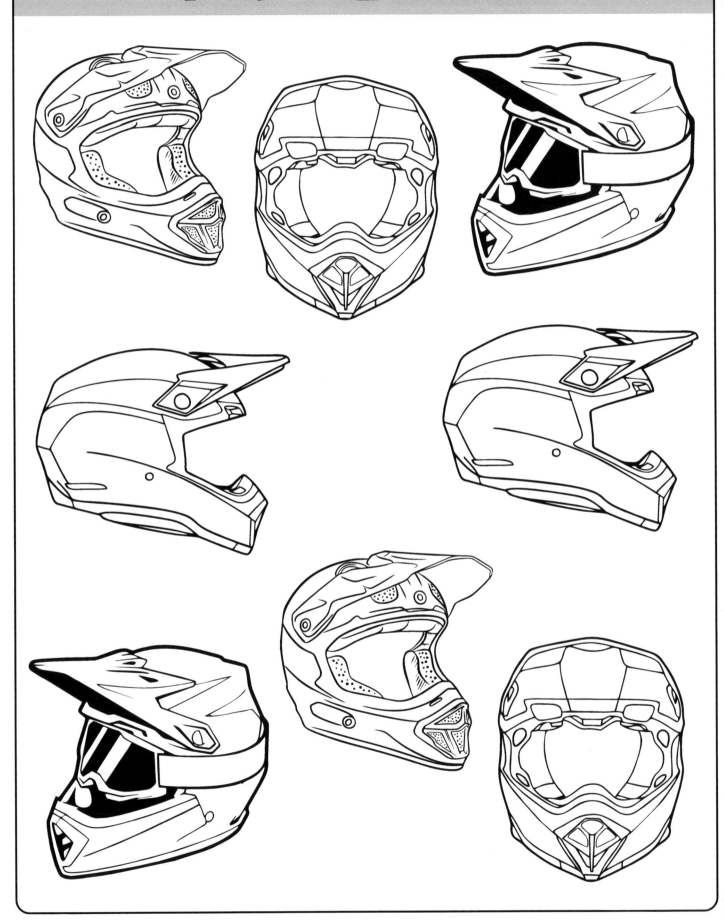

COMPLETE THE DRAWING

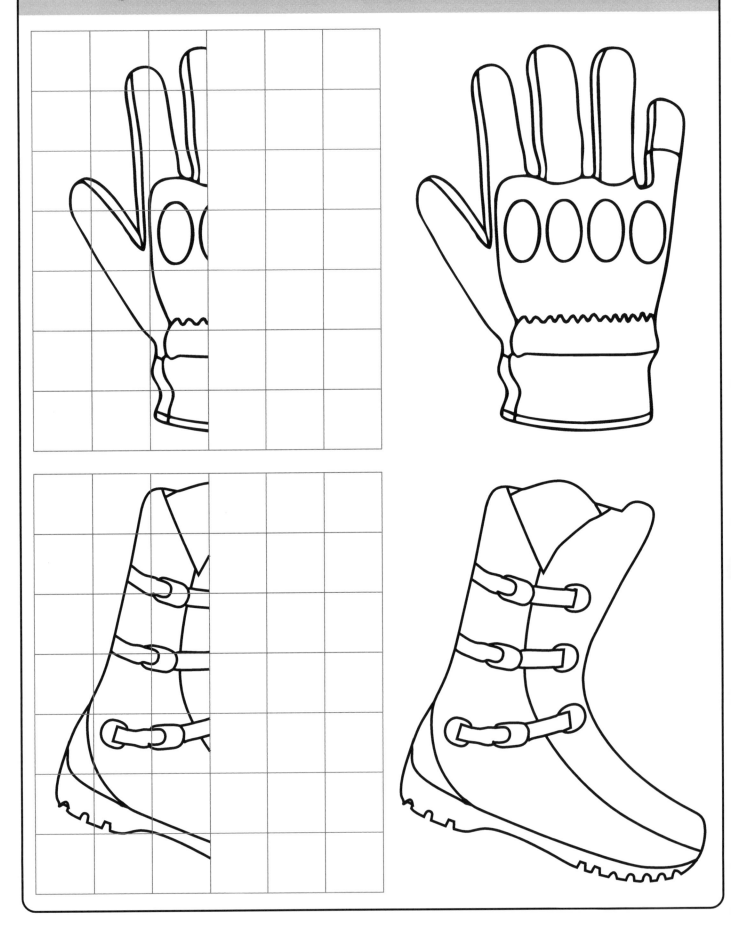

MAZE MANIA

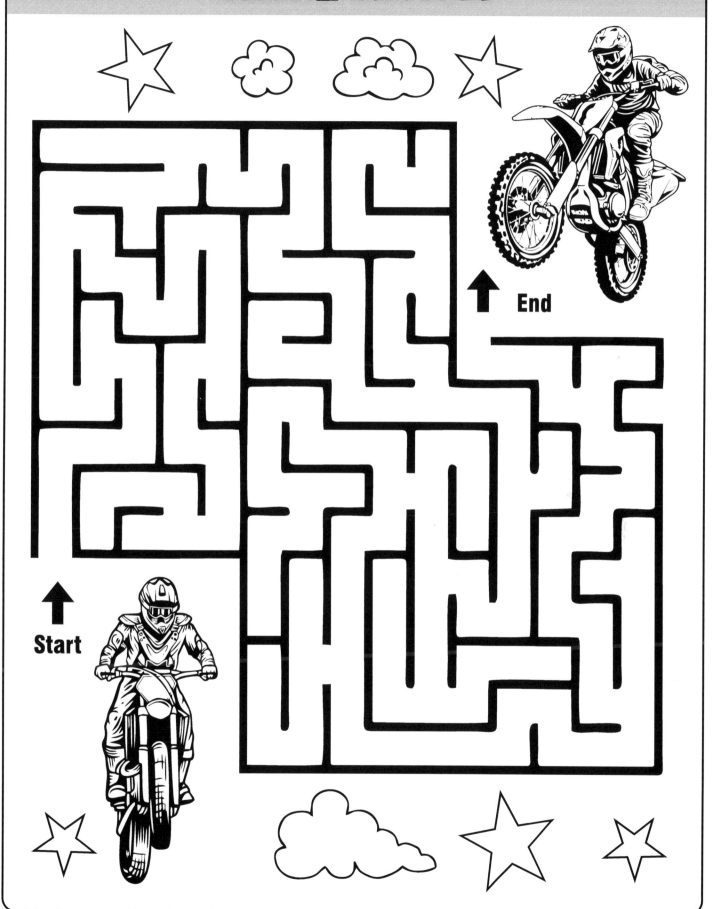

End

Start

CONNECT THE DOTS

FIND THE MATCH

COMPLETE THE DRAWING

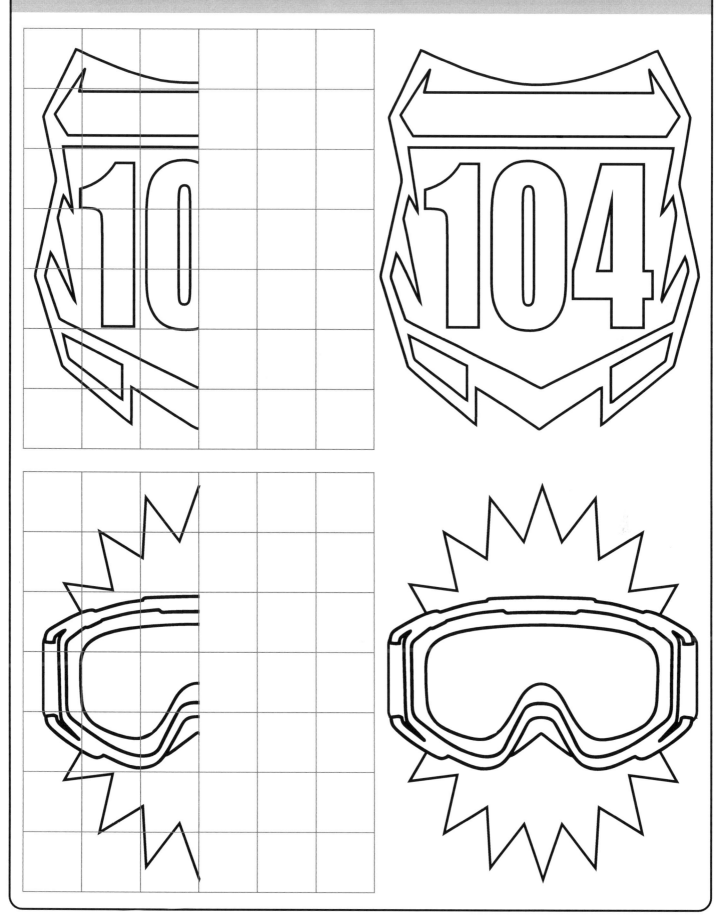

MAZE MANIA

Start

End

CONNECT THE DOTS

FIND THE MATCH

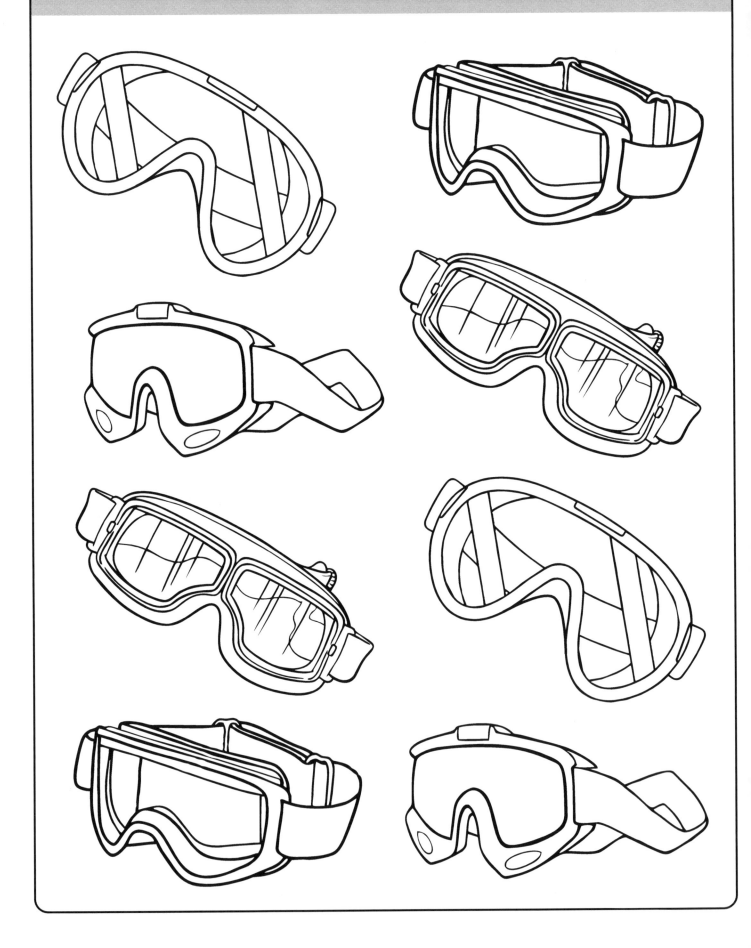

COMPLETE THE DRAWING

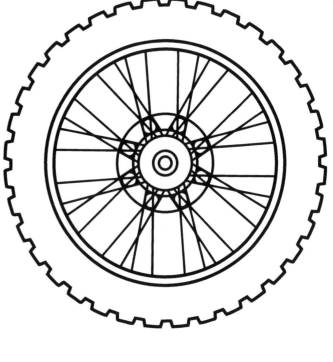

MAZE MANIA

↑ End

↑ Start

CONNECT THE DOTS

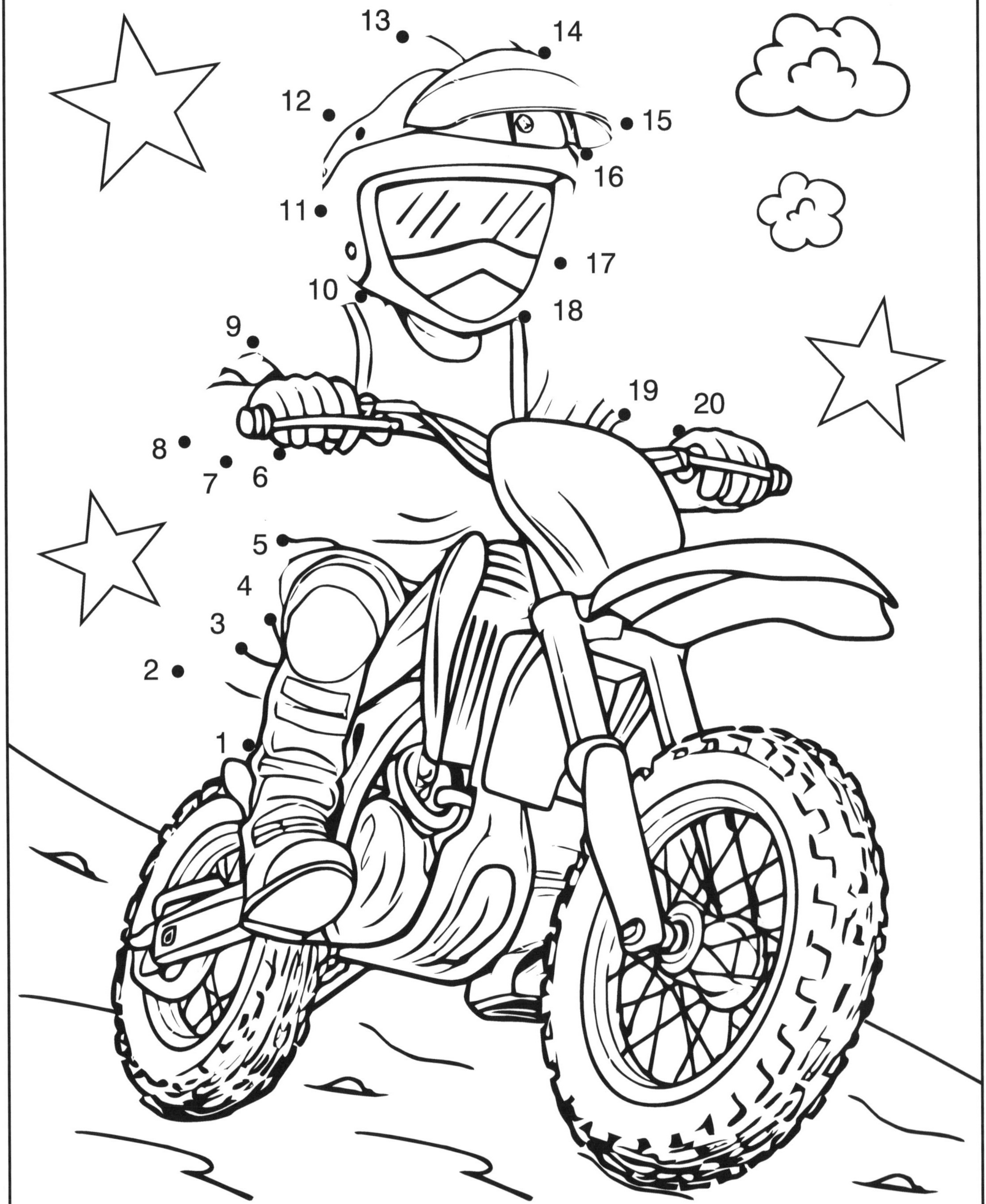

FIND THE MATCH

COMPLETE THE DRAWING

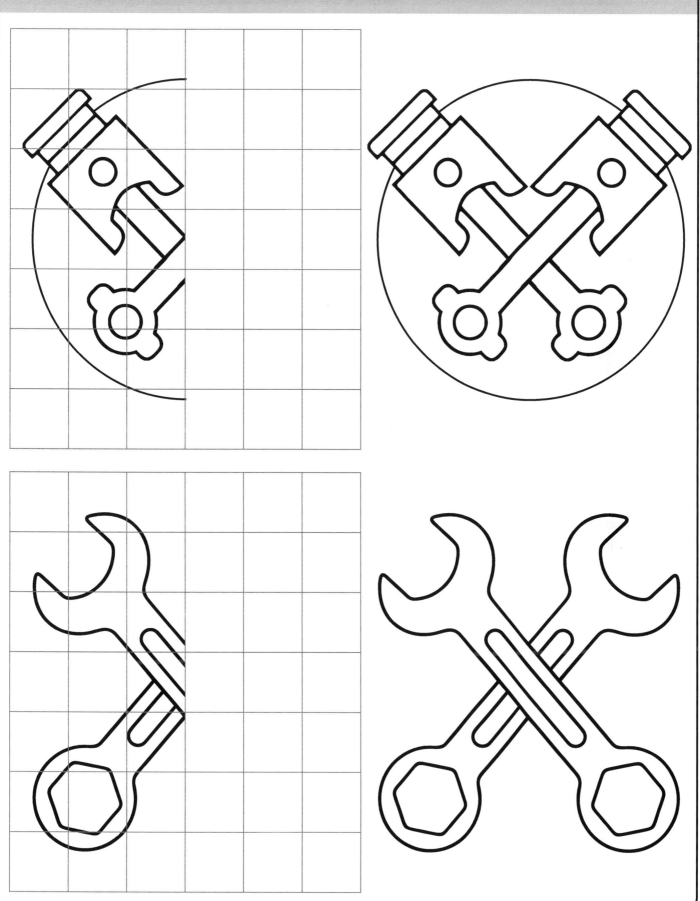

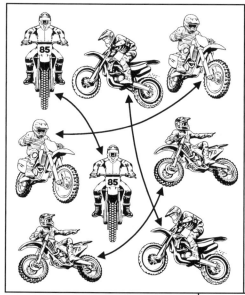

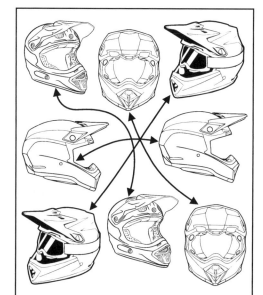

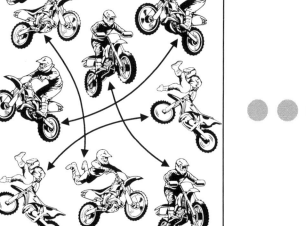
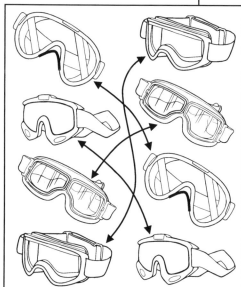

Made in United States
Troutdale, OR
03/16/2025

29800934R00018